Come into the garden, Ma

Words by Alfred, Lord Tennyson

Choral Programme Series

Consultant Editor: Simon Halsey

CLASSIC VICTORIAN BALLADS

COME INTO THE GARDEN, MAUD

TOM BOWLING · LOVE'S OLD SWEET SONG

THE SNOWY-BREASTED PEARL

THE ROAD TO MANDALAY

(SATB/Piano)

ARRANGED BY JONATHAN RATHBONE

FABER *ff* MUSIC

CONTENTS

PERFORMANCE NOTE

Choral Style

Although these arrangements are sympathetic to the original parlour songs, they are nonetheless written in a variety of styles. *On the road to Mandalay* is the most 'classical', while *Tom Bowling*, for example, is best performed in a close harmony style.

Dynamics & Rhythm

Let the music 'ebb and flow' as the Victorians might have done. A lot of music written in that period seems to us now rather self-indulgent and sentimental. Don't try to fight this – rather let it happen and **enjoy it!** Also note that the tune is not always in the soprano part, so care should be taken to make sure it can be heard when in the lower parts, for example the tenors in *Come into the garden, Maud* and *The snowy-breasted pearl*.

Words

Often the Victorian parlour song tells a narrative of some detail and so it goes without saying that the words and their delivery are very important. In general, consonants should be clear, particularly when singing the tune. Accompanying parts should, however, be aware that on occasions their words are not synchronized with the tune and therefore should be slightly less prominent. Whenever '*do*' is sung, it should have a soft '*d*' – in fact it is best to think of it as a cross between a '*do*' and a '*noo*'.

Jonathan Rathbone

This edition © 1997 by Faber Music Ltd
First published in 1997 by Faber Music Ltd
3 Queen Square London WC1N 3AU
Cover design by S & M Tucker
Music processed by Jonathan Rathbone
Printed in England by Caligraving Ltd
All rights reserved

ISBN 0-571-51813-3

To buy Faber Music publications or to find out about the full range of titles available please contact your local music retailer or Faber Music sales enquiries:

Faber Music Limited, Burnt Mill, Elizabeth Way, Harlow, CM20 2HX England
Tel: +44 (0)1279 82 89 82   Fax: +44 (0)1279 82 89 83
sales@fabermusic.com   www.fabermusic.com

Tom Bowling

Charles Dibdin
arr. Jonathan Rathbone

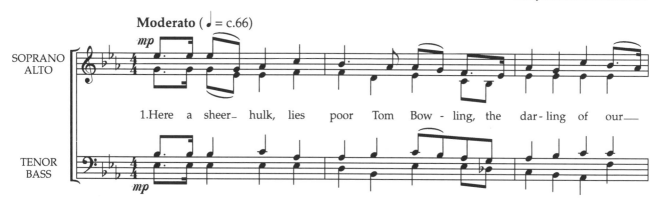

Love's old sweet song

Words by G Clifton Bingham

Music by James Lynam Molloy
arr. Jonathan Rathbone

Andante con moto ($\bullet$ = c.90)

PIANO

mf

S. *mp* Once in the dear dead days be-yond re-call, when on the world the

A. *mp* Once in the dear dead days be-yond re-call, when on the world the

T. *mp* Once in the dear dead days be-yond re-call, when on the world the

B. *mp* Once in the dear dead days be-yond re-call, when on the world the

mp

mists be-gan to fall, Out of the dreams that rose in hap-py throng,

mists be-gan to fall, Out of the dreams that rose in hap-py throng,

mists be-gan to fall, Out of the dreams that rose in hap-py throng,

mists be-gan to fall, Out of the dreams that rose in hap-py throng,

The snowy-breasted pearl

Words translated by Dr Petrie

Music Trad.
arr. Jonathan Rathbone

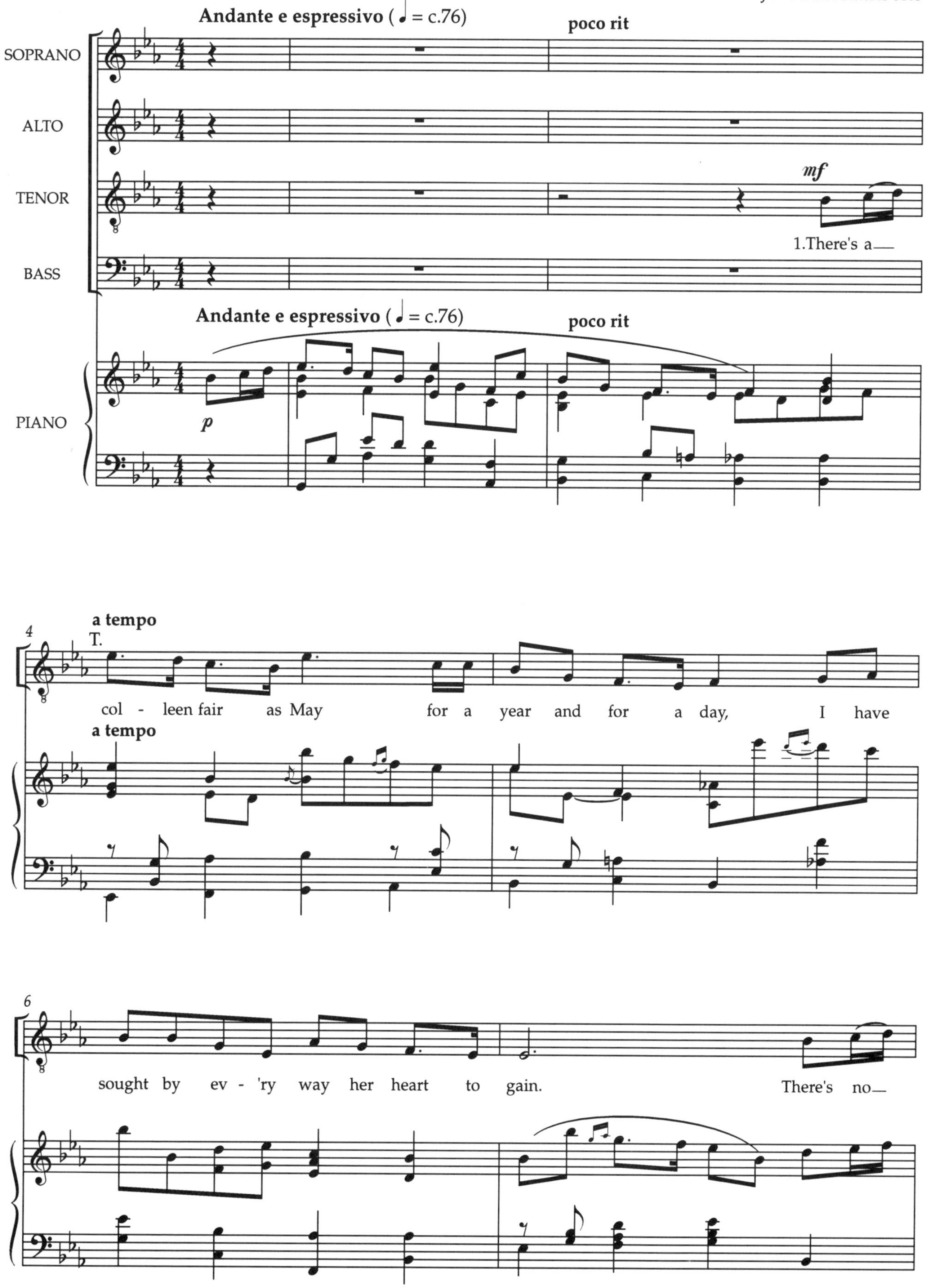

Andante e espressivo (♩ = c.76)
poco rit
SOPRANO
ALTO
TENOR
BASS
mf
1.There's a
Andante e espressivo (♩ = c.76)
poco rit
PIANO
p
4
a tempo
T.
col - leen fair as May for a year and for a day, I have
a tempo
6
sought by ev - 'ry way her heart to gain.
There's no

On the road to Mandalay

Words by Rudyard Kipling

Music by Oley Speaks
arr. Jonathan Rathbone

Lyrics:
By the old Moul-mein Pa - go - da, look-in' east - ward to the sea, there's a Bur - ma girl a - set - tin' an' I know she thinks o' me; For the wind is in the palm - trees an' the

Classic Victorian Ballads

The Victorian Music Hall era yielded some of the most enduring popular songs ever. Jonathan Rathbone's brilliant arrangements perfectly capture the inimitable style of the period, bringing this repertoire into the realm of today's mixed-voice choirs. Ideal for use in programmes and musical evenings with a Victorian theme, as popular items within any choral concert, or simply as evergreen encores.

The Faber Music Choral Programme Series

This highly acclaimed repertoire series is now a well-established programming tool for many choirs. The series, spanning both mixed- and upper-voice repertoire, offers a wealth of fresh material from the fifteenth century onwards.

With editions of the utmost integrity and practicality—keyboard reductions, singing translations and informative introductions are all included—the series aims to assist choirs, large and small, in concert programming.

Representing unprecedented value for money, each volume is a minimum of thirty-two pages and contains up to forty minutes of music.

Selected volumes for mixed voices

ISBN 0-571-51813-3

FABER MUSIC · 3 QUEEN SQUARE · LONDON
www.fabermusic.com

9 780571 518135